Eek, You Reek!

Poems about Animals That
STINK, STANK, STUNK

JANE YOLEN and
HEIDI E. Y. STEMPLE

Illustrated by
EUGENIA NOBATI

Ml Millbrook Press ◦ Minneapolis

To my stinky family! —J.Y.

For T-Waffs and the Punny Bunch—through laughter, snorts, and hilarious tears. —H.E.Y.S.

To my loving parents, Marta y Checo —E.N.

"Bang Goes the Bombardier Beetle" published as "Consider the Bombardier Beetle" © 2013, *The Poetry Friday Anthology for Middle School*. Edited by Janet Wong, Silvia Vardell

Poems by Jane: p. 4, 6, 7, 8, 13, 19, 23
Poems by Heidi: p. 10, 14, 16, 20, 21, 24, 26

Millbrook Press™
An imprint of Lerner Publishing Group, Inc.
241 First Avenue North
Minneapolis, MN 55401 USA

For reading levels and more information, look up this title at www.lernerbooks.com.

Designed by Kimberly Morales.
Main body text set in Hoosker Dont.
Typeface provided by Chank.
The illustrations in this book were created with scanned pencil drawings, textures, and Photoshop digital painting.

Library of Congress Cataloging-in-Publication Data

Names: Yolen, Jane, author. | Stemple, Heidi E. Y., author. | Nobati, Eugenia, illustrator.
Title: Eek, you reek! : poems about animals that stink, stank, stunk / Jane Yolen and Heidi E.Y. Stemple ; illustrated by Eugenia Nobati.
Description: Minneapolis : Millbrook Press, [2019] | Audience: Age 7–11. | Audience: Grade 4 to 6. | Includes bibliographical references.
Identifiers: LCCN 2018047701 (print) | LCCN 2018051180 (ebook) | ISBN 9781541560963 (eb pdf) | ISBN 9781512482010 (lb : alk. paper)
Subjects: LCSH: Animal chemical defense—Juvenile literature. | Animal behavior—Juvenile literature.
Classification: LCC QL759 (ebook) | LCC QL759 .Y65 2019 (print) | DDC 591.47—dc23

LC record available at https://lccn.loc.gov/2018047701

Manufactured in the United States of America
1-43223-33014-3/29/2019

CONTENTS

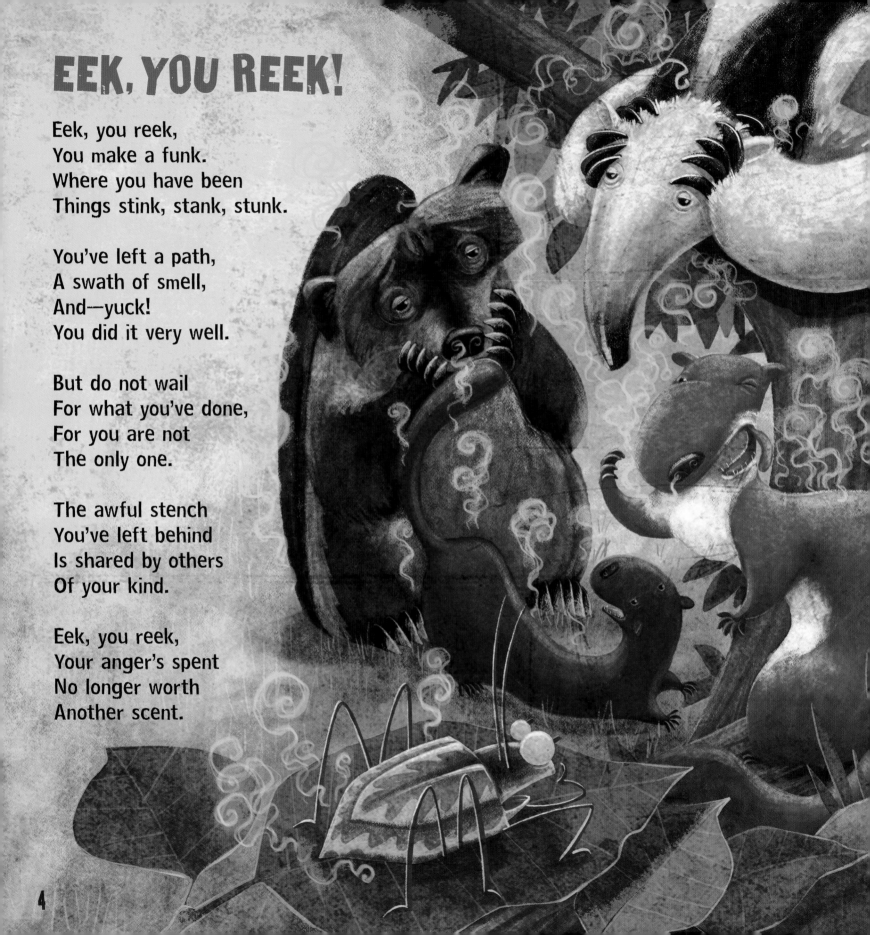

EEK, YOU REEK!

Eek, you reek,
You make a funk.
Where you have been
Things stink, stank, stunk.

You've left a path,
A swath of smell,
And—yuck!
You did it very well.

But do not wail
For what you've done,
For you are not
The only one.

The awful stench
You've left behind
Is shared by others
Of your kind.

Eek, you reek,
Your anger's spent
No longer worth
Another scent.

4

STINK STANK SKUNK

If you startle a skunk,
It can spray a big stink,
A great stench that can linger a day.
It stomps its front feet
Just to warn, lifts its tail,
And will blast anything in its way.

Some folk think that baths
In the juice of tomato
Will wash away all of the smell.
And still others say
That vanilla or soap
Or a mouthwash will do just as well.

But the skunk doesn't care.
It just wants you long gone,
And that spray is its way to go free.
So, remember, if skunks
Have moved onto your land,
Please do not send them to me.

WHO DARES EAT A SKUNK?

Great horned owls
Devour skunks.
They eat them up
In bite-sized chunks.
Because owl's got
No sense of smell,
Even foul
Can go down well.

7

BANG GOES THE BOMBARDIER BEETLE

If grabbed by a frog
Or an ant or a toad,
The bombardier beetle
Will almost explode.

BANG!

The stink it expels
Like a squirt of bug mace
Is a big, boiling blast
In the predator's face.

EATING MACHINE

If you come upon her
unforeseen,
tamandua—
ant-eating machine—
don't sneak behind her
yelling boo!
If scared,
she'll spray her stink on you.
Think you're safe?
That malodorous yield
spreads halfway across
a football field.

STINKY FERRET FAMILY AND KIN

The ferret, mink, and weasel are all kin.
They have a stink that's deep inside their skin.
And even if they like you,
And are not inclined to bite you,
Their smelliness is bound to do you in.

The ferret, mink, and weasel have a gland,
Quite full of scent their enemies can't stand.
So when they each feel frightened,
And their foe alarm's quite heightened,
They have a weapon very close at hand.

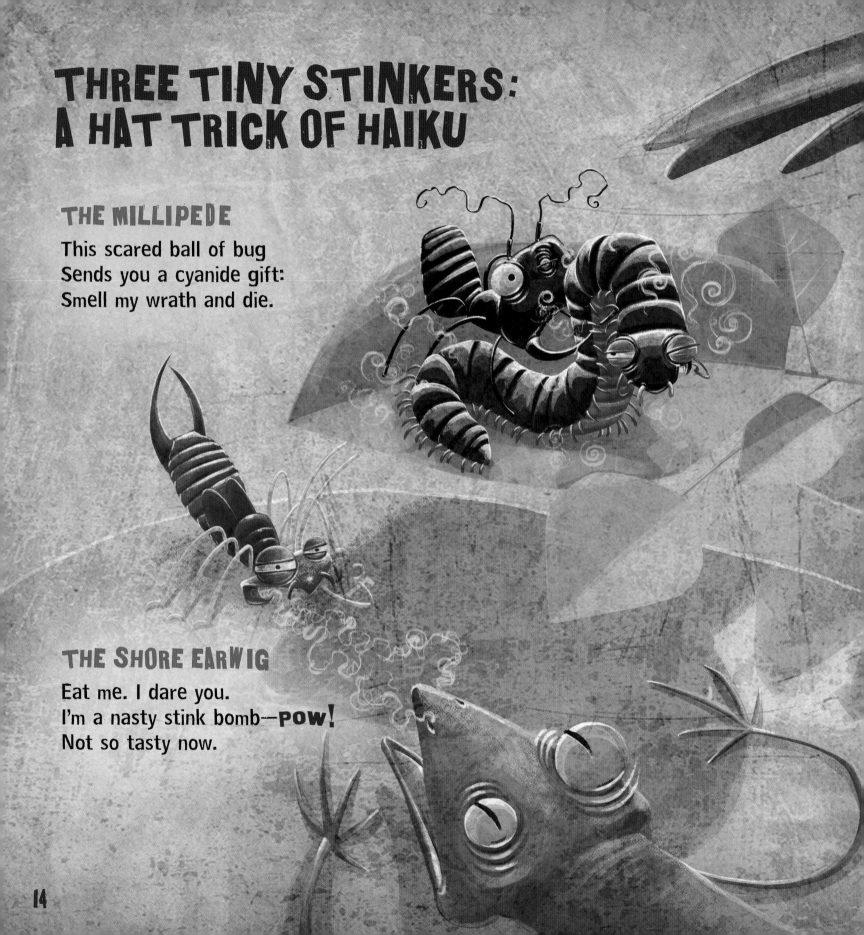

THREE TINY STINKERS: A HAT TRICK OF HAIKU

THE MILLIPEDE

This scared ball of bug
Sends you a cyanide gift:
Smell my wrath and die.

THE SHORE EARWIG

Eat me. I dare you.
I'm a nasty stink bomb—**POW!**
Not so tasty now.

THE STINK BUG

Here is my warning:
Odiferous calling card
Remains in vacuum.

TASMANIAN TEMPER TANTRUM

A fight in the night,
devils spar,
they scar.
They hunt—
alert—
forage, kill,
subvert.

A growl,
a howl,
a snarl,
teeth bared.
In the dark,
a carcass
reluctantly
shared.

The stench means
the devil
is here
to prey,
temper tantrum—
the true Tasmanian
way.

A SLOW TURTLE STINK

There you are, oh odoratus,
With your musky turtle status.
Small, mud-loving omnivore
That raccoons equally adore.

You pump out bad perfumes galore
When chased down by a predator,
Spreading stinkiness for gratis,
Little smelly odoratus.

19

STINKBIRD

In flies the hoatzin
for a crash landing,
not at all graceful—
flying or standing.

Blue face and wing claws,
Mohawk-like crest,
but what makes them odd,
is how they digest.

More bovine than bird,
eating leaves by the ton,
they chew on their cud
while they laze in the sun.

While supper ferments,
a stench fills the air.
Only the stinkbirds
don't seem to care.

WHAT EATS A HOATZIN?

Lucky for hoatzin
his cow pie bouquet
is truly unpleasant,
which makes lousy prey.

What's more, he tastes just like
his foul, fetid air.
Does he look delicious?
Then predator beware.

MAD, MEAN WOLVERINE

The largest of Mustelidae*,
He's not real nice and not real shy.
He's called a bear. I don't know why.
He really is a weasel.

He's strong, he's big, he lives in snow.
His fur is glossy. He's not slow.
But really, all you need to know
Is that he is a weasel.

He's always moving, never still.
He leaves a stench upon his kill,
So no one else will eat its fill.
He's really such a weasel.

*Mustelidae: muhs-TEH-luh-die

OX APPEAL

He doesn't worry
what you think
about his manly
oxen stink.

He doesn't worry
how you feel
about his stanky
ox appeal.

The one he's trying
to impress,
with fine fur coat
and grand largess,
is Madame Ox, who—
I confess—
loves his musky
oxen-ness.

EEK, YOU REEK, REDUX

Eek, you reek,
You've made a funk.
Where you have been
Things stink, stank, stunk.

You've warned,
You've fought,
You've found a mate.
Digested all
The leaves you ate.

And all the while,
Your putrid scent
Has made all others
Circumvent.

Eek, you reek!
You've done it well.
Keep pumping out
That awful smell.

You're odorous, gamy,
Pungent, vile,
Funky, foul, fetid—
We like your style.

STINKY ANIMALS STINK FOR A REASON

OR, RATHER, FOR ONE OF THREE REASONS

1. For defense. Whether it's a putrid spray, an explosion of foulness, or a killer gas, the smell—both off-putting and sometimes painful—keeps most predators at bay.

2. To protect food and territory. A number of animals lay down a noxious odor to keep others from their food or home. Whether it's a seeping stench or a stinky spray, it certainly does the job.

3. To attract a mate. It doesn't matter if you find the foul smell unattractive, the natural odorous cologne of a musk maker attracts the female of the species. That smell is not for you. It's for her.

SKUNK
Mephitis mephitis

You can tell if a skunk means smelly business if it stomps its front feet, raises its tail, or walks toward you stiff-legged. If so, run away. A skunk can spray up to 16 feet (5 m) or even farther if the wind is blowing. The spray can cause temporary blindness, and the smell can make you vomit. The only predators unaffected by skunk stink are owls because they don't have a sense of smell. The great horned owl—being big enough to kill a skunk—often dines on one for supper.

BOMBARDIER BEETLE
Brachinus crepitans

The bombardier beetle is slow to get off the ground, which makes it vulnerable to any earth-borne creatures that want to eat it. Over the years, the beetle has developed a very special weapon—a spectacular internal chamber. It acts as a reservoir, holding a great amount of chemical spray that is both foul and hot. The spray leaves any ant, frog, or toad that tries to grab the beetle with a sore tongue. If attacked by a swarm of ants, the beetle has the ability to spray them with its scalding fluid up to thirty times.

TAMANDUA
Tamandua tetradactyla

The tamandua (lesser anteater) of Mexico, Central America, and South America is an eating machine. One tamandua can eat almost ten thousand ants (and termites) a day. They have no teeth—their meals are ground up by their specialized stomachs. Tamanduas can use their strong arms and claws for protection, but their most effective defense is the very potent stink that they spray, like skunks, from glands located under their tails. The tamandua, however, makes skunks look like amateurs. Their stink is stronger by four to seven times, and you can smell them from 50 yards (46 m) away, which is half the length of an American football field.

FERRET
Mustela nigripes

MINK
Neovison vison

WEASEL
Mustela nivalis

Ferrets, mink, and weasels belong to the family Mustelidae, which also includes badgers and skunks. This group is well known for making a stink when scared. Mustelidae do this by releasing a secretion from scent glands to scare off any possible enemies. The males also have oil glands in the skin that produce a strong musky odor. So even if the scent gland is removed, the ferrets, mink, and weasels still smell!

MILLIPEDE
Sigmoria trimaculata

When they are scared, some millipedes not only roll up into a ball, but they also secrete a toxic and stinky liquid. No one wants to eat that! One type, the polydesmid millipede, has an extra special secretion: the lethal chemical hydrogen cyanide. They produce enough of this to kill a pigeon or mouse. Luckily, they are very small, as it would take a whole lot of scared millipedes working together to kill a human.

STINKBUG
Labidura riparia

Stinkbugs are harmless indoors when they come in to wait out the winter. Outside, they destroy many plants. They are happy to hide out of sight inside your house until spring when they want desperately to get outside. On their journey to find a way out, they are weak from not having any food and are easy to kill. But, be forewarned, if you squish them, they send out a foul-smelling substance. If you vacuum them up, your vacuum may stink for a very long time.

SHORE EARWIG
Halyomorpha halys

The shore earwig, when about to become someone's meal, spits a vile liquid from its repugnatorial glands into the would-be diner's mouth. This liquid, which smells like decomposing flesh, is a pretty good deterrent. Unfortunately, the stinky spit defense doesn't seem to work on other insects, so the shore earwig needs to rely on other defenses—mostly its clawlike forceps—to fight off buggy attacks.

TASMANIAN DEVIL
Sarcophilus harrisii

The Tasmanian devil is the world's largest carnivorous marsupial. Once native to Australia, wild Tasmanian devils now live only on the island of Tasmania. This nocturnal creature is the size of a small dog, but it is most certainly not man's best friend. On a good day, the little devil is in a foul, nasty mood. When agitated, it emits an odor worse than any skunk. Even the babies have a fighting spirit. A mama devil has more than twenty babies at a time but just four nipples for feeding. Only the strongest four survive in the mother's pouch and go on to become stinky adults.

STINKPOT TURTLE
Sternotherus odoratus

A stinkpot turtle is smaller than your hand. Nocturnal and aquatic, it has a high-domed shell that flattens as it ages. Native to the East Coast of the US and southeastern Canada as well as the Gulf Coast states, the stinkpot has four musk glands below its carapace that send out a horrible stink whenever the stinkpot tries to escape predators. That cloudlike stench works most of the time, but raccoons tend to ignore the smell and munch on the little turtles with gusto.

HOATZIN
Opisthocomus hoazin

The hoatzin is not particularly attractive, graceful, or pleasant smelling. In the swamps of South America, you can smell its manure-like odor. The smell comes from the bird's digestive system. More like a cow than a bird, it uses foregut fermentation to break down its diet of leaves, which are so low in nutrients that it needs to eat a lot. After gorging on leaves, a hoatzin will laze because the heavy meal can take days to digest. Lucky for hoatzins, they taste as bad as they smell, so no one is lining up to hunt them.

WOLVERINE
Gulo gulo

The wolverine, also known as the skunk bear, is closely related to the weasel and is part of the same family, Mustelidae. It not only sprays a strong-smelling musk on its hidden stash of food to scare off other animals, it also annoys trappers. If it finds a trap line, it will eat as many of the trapped animals as it can. Then it sprays what is left. That spray not only ruins the meat, but it also destroys the fur and keeps the traps from being used again.

MUSK OX
Ovibos moschatus

The musk ox is a big, hairy creature that stands almost 5 feet (1.5 m) high at the shoulder. Their thick fur is specialized to keep them warm in the coldest climates, which is good because they live near the Artic, mostly in Greenland and Canada. The females smell fine, but when the males are trying to attract a mate, they are very smelly. Their musky odor seems to do the job—each male ox attracts multiple partners.

A GLOSSARY OF SMELLY WORDS

BOUQUET: This should refer to the lovely smell of flowers, but in this case, it means the wafting smell of ick.

FETID: It stinks.

FOUL, FOULNESS: Like a ball gone astray in baseball, this smell is on the other side of the limits of okay.

FUNK, FUNKY: Perhaps not the highest level of stink, but definitely not right, either.

GAMY: Something that has just turned and may not make you gag, but you definitely won't want to sniff it twice.

MALODOROUS: Your odor is mal. Mal is bad.

MUSK, MUSKY: A smell that comes from an oil. Not a good oil.

ODIFEROUS, ODORATUS, ODOROUS: Filled with odor. Good or bad.

PUNGENT: Ripe. And not in a good way.

PUTRID: Something that makes you say pee-ewwwww.

REEK: To smell bad.

SCENT: For better or worse, the way something smells.

SMELL, SMELLY: Just no.

STANK, STANKY: Slang for a bad smell (or, in the case of "Stanky Leg," a dance move where you move your leg like it has gone bad).

STENCH: What wafts off something stinky and sits in the air.

STINK, STINKY, STUNK: A bad odor.

VILE: Not good. I mean, really not good. Evil.

EVEN MORE SMELLY WORDS

EFFLUVIOUS: Sneaky and invisible stink.

NOXIOUS: Bad to the toxic level.

OFFENSIVE: Makes all the nice people turn up their noses.

PERNICIOUS: So bad it causes harm or death.

PESTIFEROUS: So bad it makes you ill.

PUTREFIED: Stink that has been sitting and rotting so long it has passed beyond stinky into a new level of gross.

RANCID: Stinks because it has rotted.

REPUGNANT: So gross.

REPULSIVE: Even more so.

ROTTEN: It was once good, now it's not.

STAGNANT: Stinks because it sat too long.

FURTHER FOUL-SCENTED READING

Jenkins, Steve. *Stinkiest! 20 Smelly Animals*. Boston: Houghton Mifflin Harcourt, 2018.
Find out where stinky animals come from, what they eat, and how they distribute their terrible smell. See the ways each animal uses its smell to its advantage.

National Geographic Society. *Weird but True! Gross*. Washington DC: National Geographic, 2016.
Discover a world of nasty facts about animals, people, food, and places. Chances are, you interact with gross stuff every day! It's not recommended for reading at lunch.

Roza, Greg. *Phew! The Skunk and Other Stinky Animals*. New York: PowerKids, 2011.
Learn about how skunks and other animals make the smelly odors they use against predators. The book's photographs may help you identify—and run from—these critters in the wild.